National Anthem

Julie Murray

Abdo Kids Junior
is an Imprint of Abdo Kids
abdobooks.com

US SYMBOLS

Abdo Kids

abdobooks.com

Published by Abdo Kids, a division of ABDO, P.O. Box 398166, Minneapolis, Minnesota 55439.
Copyright © 2020 by Abdo Consulting Group, Inc. International copyrights reserved in all countries.
No part of this book may be reproduced in any form without written permission from the publisher.
Abdo Kids Junior™ is a trademark and logo of Abdo Kids.

Printed in the United States of America, North Mankato, Minnesota.

052019

092019

 THIS BOOK CONTAINS
RECYCLED MATERIALS

Photo Credits: Alamy, AP Images, Getty Images, Granger Collection, iStock, Shutterstock

Production Contributors: Teddy Borth, Jennie Forsberg, Grace Hansen

Design Contributors: Christina Doffing, Candice Keimig, Dorothy Toth

Library of Congress Control Number: 2018963342

Publisher's Cataloging-in-Publication Data

Names: Murray, Julie, author.

Title: National anthem / by Julie Murray.

Description: Minneapolis, Minnesota : Abdo Kids, 2020 | Series: US symbols |
      Includes online resources and index.

Identifiers: ISBN 9781532185380 (lib. bdg.) | ISBN 9781532186363 (ebook) |
      ISBN 9781532186851 (Read-to-me ebook)

Subjects: LCSH: National songs--Juvenile literature. | National anthems--Juvenile
      literature. | Star-spangled banner (Song)--Juvenile literature. | Emblems,
      National--United States--Juvenile literature.

Classification: DDC 973.711--dc23

Table of Contents

National Anthem

Mae stands up. Her hand is on her heart. She sings.

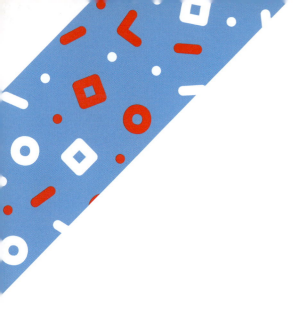

What is being sung?

The Star-Spangled Banner!

6

It is a special song.

It **honors** the U.S.

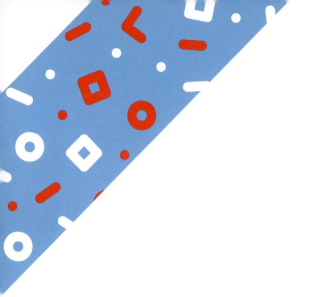

It is about a battle.

The battle took place

in 1814.

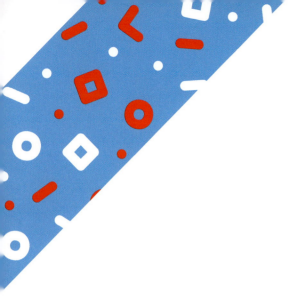

The bombs were bright.

They lit up the night.

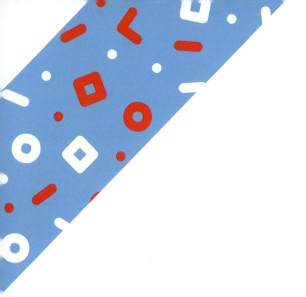

The battle ended.

The flag still stood.

Meg looks at the flag.

It is in a **museum**.

O! SAY CAN YOU SEE, BY THE DAWN'S EARLY LIGHT,
WHAT SO PROUDLY WE HAIL'D AT THE TWILIGHT'S LAST GLEAMING,
WHOSE BROAD STRIPES AND BRIGHT STARS THROUGH THE PERILOUS FIGHT
O'ER THE RAMPARTS WE WATCH'D WERE SO GALLANTLY STREAMING?
AND THE ROCKETS' RED GLARE, THE BOMBS BURSTING IN AIR,
GAVE PROOF THROUGH THE NIGHT THAT OUR FLAG WAS STILL THERE;
O! SAY, DOES THAT STAR-SPANGLED BANNER YET WAVE,
O'ER THE LAND OF THE FREE, AND THE HOME OF THE BRAVE?

Today, the song is sung at **events**. Tom holds the flag.

18

Jane is at a game.

She sings!

21

The Star-Spangled Banner

Glossary

event
anything that happens. Events can be social or important.

honor
to give respect to.

museum
a building where objects that are important to history, art, or science are kept and shown to the public.

Index

Abdo Kids ONLINE
FREE! ONLINE MULTIMEDIA RESOURCES

Visit **abdokids.com** to access crafts, games, videos, and more!

Use Abdo Kids code

UNK5380

or scan this QR code!